kalopsia

/ ka-'lop-sE-a / **noun**
the delusion of things being more beautiful than they are.

— dedicated to you

contents

open love letter

Kalopsia. I have a very lovely friend named Julia (I won't even get started on her); we see the world differently together. The world seems all mauve pink and has that old-movie-type hue over it. I romanticize the unromantic often because of her, and life seems like it holds infinite possibilities. I owe a lot of these poems to days spent by her side. But mainly the idea for this book title.

She told me one day, "We see the world like kalopsia." The definition of the word is, "the delusion of things being more beautiful than they are." I can't decide if it's intended to be a negative word? Am I supposed to apologize for this "delusion" I have?...

Well maybe they're right. Once I take off my rose colored glasses and see how the world really is, maybe this way of life has left me heartbroken or lost one too many times. But I've learned my greatest lessons this way. Does that make it worth it then? I think so.

I'd rather spend the rest of my life blinded by beauty than only ever seeing the negative. I've spent far too many days feeling alone with my thoughts and the weight of this dark world being my only friend. What has driven me to wake up in the morning is a cup of coffee and autumn air, new music on a Monday, getting to go to a quiet field in spring, baking cookies in my pj's, going antiquing for old treasures. I have lived for such small things some days they have become the only things. I hope when you read these poems you see a girl growing up and learning. I started some of the poems when I was fourteen. I was crying on my bedroom floor thinking nobody would ever read them. What's a dumb suburban kid have to say about anything? Well I'm seventeen now, and it feels like people *need* to read them. I need you in your room, lying on your childhood bed to hold these words in your hands, and find something in here, that even for a second reminds you that you're not alone.

I'm finally spilling my head, my journal, my iphone notes app to you. This is for all the teenagers afraid of themselves or hating themselves. This is for all the kids who feel like they can't exist another day. For all the ballerinas or girls who hate their bodies. For all the young lovers. For all the romantics and sad people. For all the kids questioning or confused.

You're gonna find a very lost girl in some of these pages. You're gonna find she falls in love and out of it. You're gonna find her feeling heartbroken and in pain and then you'll find she does it all over again and you'll wonder why.

Kalopsia.

That's why.

Here's to girlhood and growing.

the balance of living

there might be days when you want to
die
and you'll cry because you scare yourself

and there will be days when you can't speak
   and you'll hate the things you loved
      and you'll scream into your pillow
         and cry on the shower floor

and there will *even* be days when food won't taste like food
and your favorite snack will taste like the color grey
so you'll make friends with the growling in your stomach

and there will be days when you force yourself to sleep
in the afternoon because you can't handle your beating heart

you'll wake up glazed and puffy eyed and your mom will ask
if you've been crying

these are days that will happen
and they'll sting like your hands in the snow
and they'll feel like long car rides that never end
and they'll hurt like losing your first love did

but you'll make it to a new sunrise
 and you'll smell the crisp autumn air
   and you'll make someone laugh
      and you'll use your hands to make something beautiful
        and you'll hug your dog
           and you'll go on living despite your pain
              and while you're living you'll let yourself be proud

of how much you've grown
and you'll tell yourself good job and you'll let yourself
breathe
because you have made it through every single day of your
life so far and you'll never have to repeat another one of them
again

you only have good to look for
to *search* for
in every bookshelf
and every cup of coffee
    and every car ride
        and every person you meet from now on

and so there will be days when you want to forget
so
i want you to feel
and i want you to scream at the world
and be angry
but i don't want you to be consumed by these days

i want you to keep going
and i want you to look for the little goods that lead to the bigger ones
until they're all you *ever* see
and you'll be laughing again
    and you'll be be excited again
        and you'll forget how it felt to ever feel the opposite
you'll realize it all had to happen
for you to feel this electric right now
this sunshiny yellow
this burning orange

grasp on tightly with both hands to those feelings
(for when the next day comes and your food tastes grey)

2

these are all days that will happen
you will be both happy and sad in your life if you're like me

it's just finding *the balance of living*

2020

i need to go
get untangled
from all the things that hold me down

i need to let the universe whisper wind chimes through my ears
and tell me softly that it's possible to get past this part

i need to lay on the moist earth
remembering that i'm one of the flowers too
that i'm too **one of a kind** to be stepped on by dumb little boys

i need to breathe in new air for my lungs
go to a higher elevation
get away from these low points

i need to go

4

shell

i sat alone in the place that had meant nothing to me
now it seems it's the only thing

and i see ghosts and shells of humans i once knew wandering
the halls and sitting at the tables

i see *myself* as a memory
swinging on lampposts in love

everything moves in slow motion
so i can watch the dream pass me by

it's almost like they're walking
through me

they're so alive

maybe i'm the ghost
maybe i'm the shell of the person i was then

how love should always be

i want love like my favorite films
slow and soft
and covered in a dreamy haze

i want someone to hold my hand
 and then hold me
wrap me in their arms like it's the
only thing left to do
like if they don't do it right now
they'll die

i want someone to kiss me in the
pouring rain
make me cry with affection and
have me staring at the moon
every night because i think it's
calling me

i want the butterflies trapped in my ribcage
to be seen through my eyes
and for my lips to be so eager
to hum love songs
i'll be singing them out my window

i want someone to slow dance
to the record player with
someone to write to
someone to kiss on the cheek

i want love letters and secret kisses
and hidden hands and long hugs

audrey ann

and locked eyes and being the only
one they look for in a crowded room

to be the first one they'd think of in the
morning and the last thing they think of
before they dream

i want a love like my favorite films
but does this kind of love only exist there

first date

i took a shower and got in my towel
hair all up too
put lotion on
(my best scent)
painted my nails
while sitting in my sink
listening to the song i sent him
i lit incense and did my makeup and hair
i felt like i was in one of those
teen romance movies getting ready
for a first date
gosh i hope this goes well
this whole day i'll remember by
the scent of rose incense
our song
and mounds of fresh cream perfume

the same trap every time

i always wonder if it all still haunts you
like it haunts me
like some terribly beautiful dream
we woke up from

you answered that question
the night you laid awake apologizing to me

i'm *still* the girl you can't get out of your head
even after all the *others*

so i tell myself
that has to mean something

but i'm keeping my dreams to myself
because they'll all worry my hopes are *too* high
but i have no hopes
they are neither high nor low
i'm simply speaking the words
tattooed on my heart
the ones i've been meaning
to read aloud
and wherever they lead me
i'll have no other choice
but to follow

my own selfless mistake
over the *same* selfish boy

boys like stardust

i tried to fill up on boys
like stardust

pretty
 shiny
  dreamy
   all consuming

unreachable really
but none of them had me oozing poetry from my lips
and singing love songs out my window

my mouth ran dry
hands cramped

tired from writing about
you

mom's melon candle

you know when you wake up early in the summer
before the rest of the world and before the heat has time to set in
you creak down your stairs and the golden sun is falling all over the house
and you open the windows or you step foot outside to the still air
and the birds talk through your chimney
and the world smells like *melon* and sea salt
and your body can't help but move in the golden sun so you waltz in your kitchen
with coffee bound to spill

it's that simple beauty i only take note of in dreams or on winter days
once they're long gone and i've almost forgotten
how beautiful it all was

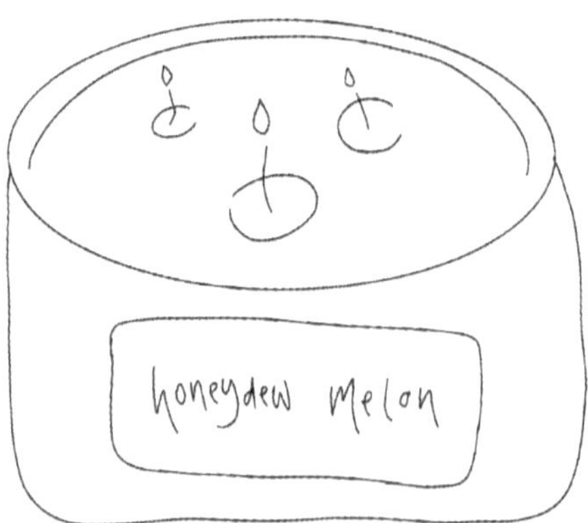

to do

burn your skin off in a hot bath
or go numb
from making snow angels all day long
<u>i don't know</u>
but oh my gosh
please
do whatever it takes to feel some
release

mary oliver

you made me put my *lips to the world*
you made me watch sunsets
you made me sing out your car window
you made me run through fields
you made me praise the
sky
you made me read poetry
aloud
you made me cry
you made me laugh
you made me who *i am*

i am only me because of
you

i was only half a girl
before you

13

hands down

my heart was so full
and my legs felt electric
our knees touched
i looked at him
smiling
hands down by the greeting committee plays
our fingers intertwined
then locked
my body was a whole heartbeat

i feel so good when i'm with him

february

it's only the start of february

but i'm falling in love with a boy
who called me a dream

i am on every cloud nine
there ever was

i feel like i'm
floating

cough syrup

i felt the way you feel when you're
on the verge of a sickness
your body aches for no reason

i felt the way you feel when you've
been in a hot tub for too long
hazy and drained

except i wasn't sick at all
and i hadn't been in a hot tub since may

i was just numb
so numb

and you can't take cough syrup for that
and you can't just see the family doctor for that

and you can't just stand up and get out of the water
whenever you please for that

you are trapped

inside of yourself

in a year

if in a year we've broken each others hearts

at least

we had today, we had now

and maybe that's all we need

and maybe that's all that matters

because we are both lost souls helping each other

so

if in a year we've broken each others hearts

i can only hope it's because we're both not lost souls anymore

keep growing

i do not miss you anymore
i only miss the person i was then

maybe i should just keep growing
keep trying to love the new me
stop trying to reach an old
unattainable
picture of myself
with you

headache

my head hurts
from crying
from mourning over lovers
still here on earth

but

        so

             far

                  from

                       me

getting better

i am both
the messiest i've ever felt
and the happiest i've ever been

i am still trying to figure out how that is

hello old feelings

all of the sudden you were all i could think of again
you have power over my thoughts
and i wish i wasn't this easily consumed
trust me
but i want you so bad my heart feels like
it's scraping my insides
yelling to get out
to run back to you
to have you hold me
to hear you say my name again

they still waltz when i don't

i was so sad today it felt like i was drowning myself and pulling at my hair and
clenching my fists and screaming into my pillow *all alone*

but i wasn't doing any of those things
and i wasn't alone
i was surrounded by people

i stood there with glazed eyes
staring at the walls as they waltzed

audrey ann

you're always thinking of her

we listen to the same music
the only difference is
you're always thinking of her
and i'm always thinking of *you*

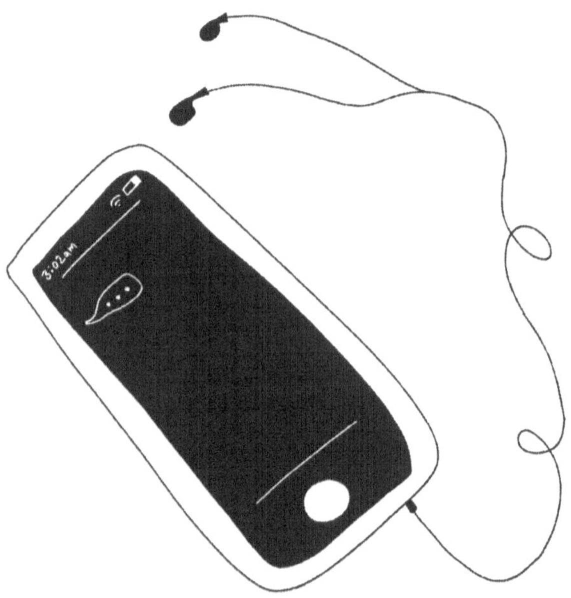

polaroid

it's hard to hear you talk about lovers you wished loved you

to hear you yearn and ache and wish

for someone to come running to your window

to make you come alive

when that's all i've ever done

all i've done is cry and scream into pillows over you

all i've done is ache all over when you speak

alll i've done is study your wrists

all i've done is write you letters i'll never slip under doors

all i've done is hold on tight to perfect images

of us in days captured like film

i remember us now how we looked in your polaroid then

we are nostalgic for days we've lived and you yearn

for lovers who already love you

full for once

i'm so full of life for you

you make me hum love songs in the ice cream aisle

you make me dance in the streets at night

you make me swing on lampposts like they do in old romance movies

25

late may

it's the sound of rain out her window late may

it's the way the sun danced off her eyes on the train

it's how we laid there under the trees reading

it's her head falling on my shoulder when she laughs

it's my legs holding her feet up after walking all day

it's our knees pressing together

it's our hands touching on accident

it's her singing in the car softly

it's her hair blowing about with the windows down

it's all made me adore her you see

oh i wish you could see her

end of july

words spill out of my mouth

and ooze from my skin at the sight of a july day

spent in the sun

admiring the light slipping through the trees

and onto her skin

my thoughts end as scribbled entries on humid nights

the heat clinging to my lips

i can taste the salt from pool days behind me

i don't know where summer went

but the sound of the birds out my open window make me wander far off

audrey ann

the woman i wished to be

i become more like the woman i wished to be every day

i wear golden rings

and keep mints in my bag

car keys in my pocket

and wear a signature perfume

i try to make my bed every
day

and do my hair nicely

wash my clothes on friday

and wear a new lip color

i buy myself coffees

and read books for pleasure

take the long way home to hear my one song

and wear mom jeans

i buy big earrings

and hang posters on my walls

listen to oldies radio

28

audrey ann

and cut my own hair

i become more like the woman i wished to be everyday

her

i am consumed by her

i am consumed by all of her being

picture your life for me

i'm not sure i realized until recently

why my heart ached

until i pictured myself old and grey and sitting selling stories from days like these

who would i want to say i did it all with?

i want to tell them you

because

i don't want to see paris with another

i don't want to rome italy alone

i don't want to move to the south of france without you

i don't want to lay in the fields, staring at the sky if you're not tangled in the flowers along with me

i don't want to sing my favorite songs without you

i don't want to hold another hand

or kiss some other lips

or cry into anyone else's shoulder

or slow dance in anyone else's arms

i don't want to live unless i'm by your side

i don't want to experience this world without you

i could say you are all i see when i picture myself old and grey

but really you are all i ever see

any day, any time, any place

you are all i ever see

audrey ann

i do, i do, i do

i wish someone would write about me like this she said

"someone does"

she didn't believe me but she was all i wrote of today

audrey ann

still yours

my heart is still yours if you want it

it's up for grabs

hanging by the hooks on the back of my door

waiting to be picked in the garden beside my house

sent in a letter and sealed with a kiss straight to your door my dear

it's still yours

i question it all now

what was rushing through your head when i sat under the patio

rain falling around us

as i read you pages from my heart

were you already planning your escape

were you already planning on ripping the pages out

were your words already an empty glass by then

or was i just draining you out

when i whispered three words in your ear and you whispered them back

were you already lying

 or did you mean them then

you have left me questioning

everything

lying to myself

i have lied

i've pictured me in your arms once more and your hand in mine everyday since i saw you last

i have the overwhelming sense you're all i need

but i'm afraid my heart doesn't always know what's in my best interest

you are unreliable and easily breakable

at one point or another i thought i held you together quite nicely

but i wasn't enough

how could i possibly pick your pieces up now when i'm just as shattered?

to let love in only to know it's bound to break you once more is foolish i know

but the middle bit where i'm in your arms again might be worth it all

but the middle bit where your hands are on my waist and we're dancing to our favorites songs again might be worth it all

but the middle bit where i kiss you fearlessly and like i mean it finally might be worth it all

maybe i need a second chance so that it's all worth it

i'm just hoping your not in love with someone else already

36

i'm just hoping i'm the girl who made you forget all the others

i'm just hoping you'll come back to me soon

because

summer is dissolving before our eyes and all i can see is you

only you

even after all these months

audrey ann

clair de lune

i've been trying to forget you

but i've done an awful job

because i'm crying once more at clair de lune

the art of missing you

i miss you

i miss your little laugh you hated

i miss you silly curly hair and how it looked golden in the sunlight

i miss your eyes and how they looked that night in the rain

i miss your hand

mine has nothing to hold now

i miss the way you made me laugh when i'd cried all the nights before

i miss the way you made me feel

it was like everything would be infinitely okay because i had you

i miss loving you

i miss being in love with you

i miss you

will i ever stop

audrey ann

things you'll learn

he'll call you his dream a month prior

he'll be anxiously waiting to call you his love weeks before hand

you'll be dancing around your room to love songs and smiling at your phone

you'll look through old poetry books to find love letters you can finally relate to

but then he'll change his mind overnight

then he'll be anxiously waiting to call you his ex

you'll skip every love song you sent him and scream lyrics you never used to get in the car without hesitation

you'll look back at the poetry

and all the the times before when you said you never understood the heartbroken girl who wrote them

you'll be underlining her words with permanent marker

wondering how it's possible for things to change *this fast*

40

summer love

i deserve a love that feels like summer all year-round

damaged love letter

i told you in a perfume sprayed letter

stamped in my lips

that it was true we may not last but that at least we had today

that at least i loved you today

i should have lied

i shouldn't have been so vulnerable

i think it gave you the courage to leave

42

think of me when the sky is pink

think of me when the sky is pink and the water is blue

one day you'll see the ocean again

and the color of my eyes will flood your mind

one day you'll see a pink sky

and you'll want to tell me all about it

but one day you'll hear our song on the radio

and you'll sing it to another girl the way you did to me

but it's alright

the ocean and the sky will still serve as reminders of me

audrey ann

just wondering

what did you do with my painting on your desk?

our framed photo from february?

the heart shaped nonsense?

the love letters?

the playlist i sent you?

do i fill your recently deleted?

audrey ann

hunger kills ya know

i'm so hungry

for some masterpiece of a romance

i never quite got from you

audrey ann

learn learn learn and continue

and my heart has had to learn

no matter how good you think you are to someone

or for someone

they will not always

be good in return

audrey ann

cheap cologne

you smelled of january nights and coffee shops at noon and holding hands in the movies and painting on the lawn that spring

but on second thought

maybe you just

smelled like *a boy*

i can't explain much else

it was just *sweet innocence* and a new *cheap cologne* fogging my image of you

back to reality

and love songs are just songs again

and warm summer days aren't ours anymore

and the midnight sky isn't full of shooting stars for us to wish on now

and you are no longer my morning muse or afternoon daydream *in fact*

you haven't filled my dreams in weeks

life went on after us just when i thought it never would

and you have just become another boy to me

us but in summer

i miss us in summer

i thought we'd be okay

but i feel so far away from you

it's hurting me physically

i'm crying on some random tuesday night in september

now my head is pounding and my cheeks are wet and eyes are puffy

already

i'm *already* like this

i thought i'd at least make it until winter

i wish i could go back in time and have you look at me like i was an angel

like i put the very sun in the sky

i wish i could go back in time to laying in your bed laughing

i wish i could back in time to watching the sunset beside you

49

or reading poetry by the water or the day we got lost missing our exit

or the time you couldn't wait to drive to my house that one july evening

or the time you danced with me all night to the same damn song

all of it

i want it all back

even who i was then

whoever that is

in a world of my own

life is a beautiful

beautiful

tragedy

so i play classical music through my room

late at night and stare at my walls

romanticizing the unromantic

it seems to be the only way to live

laying on the ground letting music

rip me to pieces

it makes things more bearable

if it all feels like a dream

audrey ann

you were right

the girl who writes poetry

has always written about you

and the girl who bakes pastries

has always baked them for you

and the girl who dances

has always danced for you

and the girl who reads

has always read to find you

and the girl who runs

is always running to you

and the girl who paints

is always painting you

and the girl who sings

is always singing to you

you're too blind to notice

but she's madly in love with you

it's all been for you

quite a silly girl really

wasting all her time

wasting away over you

maybe she should start doing those things for herself

if you love me leave a clue

i still listen to your playlists

check up on your new ones

make sure you aren't leaving me any clues in the music

it's embarrassing

and i'm stupid for caring this much

but i'm also too much of a romantic

to let the small hope that you did leave me clues

pass me by

so i go on listening

trying to hear you speak in songs you didn't write

trying to listen for lyrics that tie us back together

it's humiliating

it's lonely

only hearing you through someone else's voice in my earbuds

oh spring

don't you ever just lay on the ground and stare at the sky and the birds that fly and the way the sun hits the green trees

i'm looking at them now and i can't help but think this is all there is

and all there needs to be

me and the trees

me and this picture of a wonderful world where birds sing and sunlight is golden

don't you ever?

love

there is no real way to explain the depth of the word

love

it seems hollow and empty and overused

but

one day you will feel love

on your lips

one day you will hold love

in your arms

one day you will look at love

in the eyes

one day love will be the only feeling left in your bones

or the only one that matters

it's unexplainable

it's the blood rushing through your body

it's the sunlight on your face and fireworks on the fourth of july and the moment your favorite artist enters the stage

it's the loveliest beginning

the ultimate climax

and the happiest ending

it's like green grass sprouting in the spring from your stomach and butterflies in your rib cage and flowers growing right out in between it all

it'll make you come alive again

ballet studio

i love this place

in a somewhat different way than you're expecting

i love the bodies that fill it

i love the way the sun peeks through the wooden window frames

and casts a spotlight on our faces

i love these floors that feel like
they root me like a tree into the
earth

i love these barres that have
held many hands

i love these walls that have
heard many laughs and cries
and silent whispers

i love this place

in a somewhat beautiful way

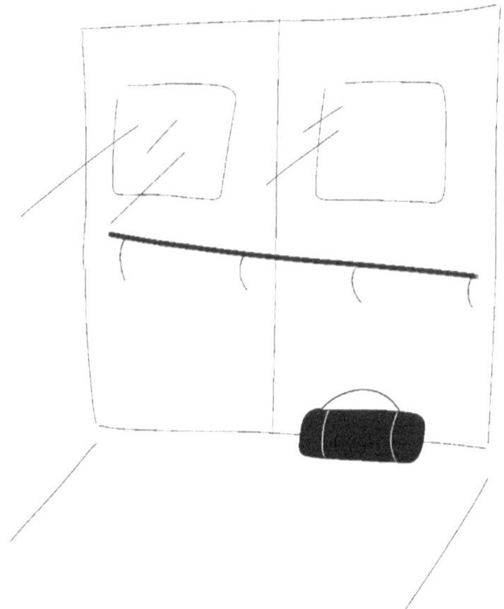

59

moderate to severe

i can't even save myself when i'm depressed
when my moderate depression turns into severe depression
i can't even remember how to save myself
things that inspired me no longer make me want to run through sunflower fields
with a paintbrush in hand singing my favorite songs
and things that made me laugh no longer leave my stomach sore
and things that i loved feel like chores
and i can't even get out of the house to drive and breathe and feel the air and sun
on my skin because i'm too sad
and everything that made me come alive has lost all its color
so on days when my moderate depression turns into severe depression
i forget everything that helps me feel like *me*
i unlearn every coping skill and positive affirmation
i just wait it out
i try to believe that time will heal me best it can

an ode to july

it's july 31st at 11pm and i feel every laugh, tear, and moment of this last month on my skin

what a lovely mess of a month july always is

july is summer

it's fireworks

pool parties

friends

bike rides through fields of green

lanterns and s'mores

campfires outside

my house smells of pineapple candles

and i'm always hit with the breeze of my old fan

it's strawberry stained tongues and vanilla ice cream cones

it's when i am most whole

so it pains every bone in my body to say farewell for another year

i go quite mad without july

audrey ann

it's sticky but sweet and always leaves too quick

farewell july

mid-march

and i was running up a hill mid-march

with my arms afloat behind me

sprawled out

they felt like bark on a tree peeling right off my worn body

this new spring air is damp

like a new summer dress fresh out the
wash

the grass is tickling my thumbs green

and i'm still running

the air is choking me but i haven't gotten a
breathe like this since

july

the smell of rain is still in the air

the world has a haze of yellow and green
on now

she's so lovely in yellow and green

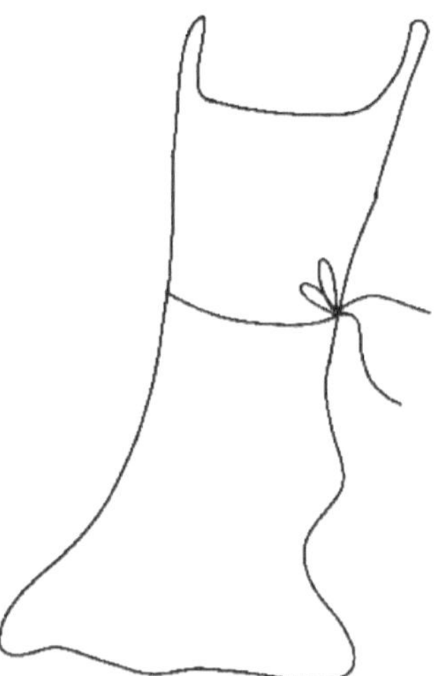

audrey ann

who am i

let me tell you

i am not what you see online

i am far from that girl

i am not my clothes

i am not my things

i am not my views or likes

i am not my house

i am not my friends

i am not my dancing

i am not my hair

i am not my makeup

i am not even merely my skin and bones

i am not

(nor do i need to be)

defined by any of those things

i am fearfully and wonderfully made by my God

that i know

i know that i am my heart, my soul, my laugh

and however i choose to dance around a room when no else is watching

i am however i sing when no one else is listening

i am all the random things that make me

me

i am loved by the Holy Spirit

that i know

i no longer need to be defined and stereotyped and put into a box for others to decide what to do with next

i am worth more than that

(*you my dear reader are worth more than that*)

so to answer the first question i gave you

who am i?

i am His.

i should be crying

i want to cry
it feels like it's the *right* thing to do

but maybe i've cried over these wounds too many times now
i've hurt this hurt now enough to where it doesn't leave me with anything

it's my routine now
i'm just constantly feeling

so tears are long gone
it's just emptiness

thinking of you

the thought of you melts my insides
sends butterflies swarming in my stomach
makes me breathe in a little deeper
flowers even smell sweeter
just by thinking of you

audrey ann

i know i know i know

i know that the river doesn't stay frozen over forever
that winter will end and i'll feel summer heat again
but that doesn't mean the cold isn't still just as bitter on my skin

audrey ann

mind on fire

i can not turn my mind off
i've laid in bed for hours this week
trying to sleep
to escape
but every time i just ache all over
thoughts eat me alive as i lay there
i'm yelling in silence
it's the most painful thing in the world
aching to escape yourself
to jump out of a window and run
to find who you used to be
and i don't want to talk about it
i don't want to write about it
so i just continue suffocating
it's all so exhausting
i stare in the mirror trying to find a reflection
i stand in crowded rooms and feel the loneliest i've ever been
i stand there feeling dizzy or like death has come over me
like if i don't run out of the room and collapse onto the floor and
bawl my eyes out right this instant
i'll never breathe again
but i never run out of the room
somehow
i hold myself back all by myself
it's my biggest accomplishment of the day
not letting myself go

70

never enough for me

why can't the romance of lying under the moonlight in my own white metal bed frame be enough for me?

why must i always want

i am lit by the moon tonight
this other world shines on me
giving me its grace and peace
yet i am ungrateful and full of hunger
for a light that burns in a boy who
doesn't love me anymore

audrey ann

71

to: myself

longing will kill you
i know it will be hard to stop loving them
to stop wanting them
to stop imagining what life would look like with them

but put down the famous romance poet
and don't watch the rom com
and don't listen to love songs about how she'll love him her whole life

you have to stop holding on at some point
because it will kill you
and drive you mad
and make you lose sight of how love should *feel* and *be*

you shouldn't be chasing love
and you shouldn't be begging for attention from love
and aching through your whole body for love
quit your romanticized longing for once and

let
   them
      go

before you let yourself go

february

i will always have this romantic need and longing in me
that is just me
but for the first time in a long time the trees and the breeze and the warm sunlight
on my skin and in my eyes feels like enough
and i'm alone
i'm alone and i'm content with that
i should really get out and see the sun more
i feel like something just broke inside me
like the sunlight burst right through me
i'm warm inside now
it's 65 degrees on february second
like some mini spring
whispering that she's close
if you just keep holding on
(and i just might!)

and there is something about listening to classical music while you do the most
mundane things in your life that is so romantic
it almost saves your life entirely
so today i am thankful for the first bit of sun on my pale skin this year
and music that makes you want to live again

i'm at the park right now having a little date alone
i'm laying on a hill by the water on some old blanket
i packed food and books
i can't help but lay here observing and dreaming
doesn't it make your heart swell seeing two lovers together
or an old man alone on a park bench
or a woman fresh from a run sitting admiring the water

today is just good

last week i cried almost everyday and slept many hours trying to numb the pain
of living and i couldn't seem to turn my mind off for one second
but
that was just a bad week
it is not a bad life
things are looking up and i'm feeling better
those are just days i will have
but i stay alive for ones like today

don't make me fall for you

i'm extreme
so loving you will consume me
your golden skin will melt me still in the colder months
your hazel eyes will make mine cry
your voice singing me love songs will echo in my head
until the end of time

i only love in extremes
and i know you won't be able to
so darling *don't make me fall for you*

audrey ann

kiss her

do you kiss her because she's in arms reach?
or do you kiss her because she means something to you?

either way i hope you kiss her and wish it were me

i'm very tired

please let me be
please let me sleep under the stars for once
without picturing myself in your arms

audrey ann

carbon copy

if i can't have you
i'll just take parts of you
and find them in new lovers

i'll find your smile tangled in some other boys
and that'll be enough for me

i'm tolerable

others have made me weakened
softened my edges
as i cut around their corners
and bled on my knees

i like the way you build me up
and i like the way i let myself grow in your vicinity
i am new in your eyes
i am untouched and tolerable

pinch me

i strive for a love that will make me stop in my tracks ten years down the line
and ask myself

has this all been a dream
and for my love to have to come pinch me

facetime

i was stupid for calling you
dancing around your room
but what else am i to do but waste my time watching you

you kept giving me this drunken sideways grin
it spread across your whole face

you said i was the most beautiful girl you've ever seen
you said the moment you first saw me you fell in love
i laughed and smiled and threw it all over my shoulders
like you were reading me a script
like you were reading me lies

but is it true
that drunken words are sober thoughts

could you love me for real in another life
could you love me now if 800 miles took you a minute to walk
could you love me now just because you love me *right now*
and not just because you've been drinking

audrey ann

lovers who never love me

i keep falling in love with lovers
i keep listening to their aching hearts
longing for someone else

and i listen and tell them there's beauty in seasons of waiting
but nobody ever gives advice
without having gone through the very battle
themselves

so every lover i love has never loved me
and i wonder some days if anyone has ever thought of me in ways i dream
and if nobody has what does that mean

i'm a vessel of aches and pains
from holding many broken hearts
not just my own
i want to stop holding onto them all someday

i'd drop everything

i'm really not sure how i'd be if i didn't know you
it feels like i've had to know you
there is no life anywhere
no alternate universe
where i don't know and love you
i've never cared about another human being
without any second guessing like i do for you

i'd drop everything most days just to run to listen
and or be with you
sometimes that scares me
i was meant to know you and it's so crazy
how much i love you
i hope you know that always

pandemic

the world is imploding
falling to bits before us
but you and i
still come together to dance
and speak about books
that make us fall to the floor
(you make me fall to the floor)

so the world is ending
and the best of us could die tomorrow
so if you prefer me to call you love
i won't dare hesitate

i could spend the rest of the time i have on earth
searching for you in poems
just to send them all to you

that funny feeling

it's early sunday morning
and my stomach feels weird
and my hands are a bit shaky
and my whole body aches
for you

i believe half my heart longs for you always
and the other half is already yours

so why can't i run to your window in my gown
and shove flowers down your throat until you're in my arms

because the thought of dying sounds better
than losing our summers under the trees
over me stumbling on my words

i'll go on imaging your lips on mine
i'll go on pretending you are nothing more
than my platonic love
i'll go on
because without you i fail to be here
i fail to be anything worth knowing without you
i only want to be known with you

for someone who misses summer

it's late at night
i'm lying in the grass with warm company
and a full day in my past
leaving me feeling filled to the brim
there's a smell of kids running in the streets
and jumping in pools
and licking ice cream that falls
onto sticky hands in the air
the lanterns fill my blind spot
the fireflies flicker off and on
the thought of grabbing a jar
and running around my yard catching them
all passes through my mind
but soon goes to marshmallows and
campfires
i smell one down the street
and for some reason i can actually see the stars in the sky tonight
i didn't think that was possible anymore
i can hear the bugs
and i am in love
with nobody in particular but life itself
and i'm lying in the grass still
letting myself leave a mark into the earth
(and possibly stain my white shorts green)
this
this is summer
this is july
it smells of pineapple and open windows and salty pools mixed with sunscreen
these things i miss on a freezing day in february

audrey ann

stop teasing

you keep teasing the idea of running to throw rocks at my window

the thing is

i've spent many nights holding myself back from doing just that

except i'm never teasing

i'd run to your window in a heartbeat

hands

what do i do with my hands if not place them in yours
or use them to hold your head up high
or wipe your tears

tell me
what are these hands good for if not holding you

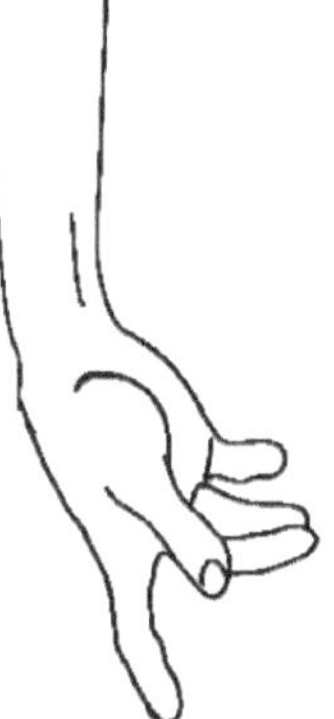

if i started i'd never stop

i feel it all welling up inside me
like i'm choking down all my words
and holding back floods of tears
if i don't tell you everything
i'll collapse soon
and you keep speaking in poems
and telling me you love me when i laugh
and i can't stop blushing or put two words together
to even thank you
because i'm afraid if i said it back this time i wouldn't be able
to shut my mouth from spilling i love you's in ways you've only
dreamed
i'd melt right over
on to you
and it's all welling up inside me
the greatest ache i've ever held

you speak so confidently about things i only imagine late at night
so when you're so cool
and i'm tangled in my words
know it's not because i disagree
or i can't give enough to you
but i don't respond to you in the ways i know you want
because everything you say
all of it
is so real
too real for me
that i can't laugh or joke or pass it off as nothing
aching all for you is too real
crying all for you is too real

because sometimes i think i've given it all to you
all of me
there's not a bit of me you haven't traced with you own finger

i tell the moon about you

and one day
you'll know

and all the nights spent grieving over a youth spent alone
and wishing someone would kiss your hands
or lay with you in your bed of soft flowers
won't feel like sun soaked day dreams from summers past

because darling
all the nights i listened to you cry to the stars
and mourn over nothing
i stayed up after with the moon telling her
how my heart beats for you

i tell the moon about you

audrey ann

breaking point

if someone were to tap me i'd shatter
into a billion pieces for them
crack right down the center
let them put me back together

i feel so far away from people on earth
i'm on a another planet
here there is no gravity
i float in the universe

i'm so numb
i notice my tears are warm
they are warm against my pale skin
they almost burn

every word i speak is heard as if through closed doors
i'm screaming but i don't let anyone hear me

i'm not even sure the image in the mirror is myself anymore
she's cold and hollow and hates herself
it's like i'm staring into the face of my fears
and she screams at me and then i just stare blankly back

tears wash my face
no need for soap and water

i'm so tired of her
i'm so tired of myself

92

thanks for not eating me alive

some days
when i remember
i stretch my body out on a spring morning
arms and chest pointed to the sky
i breathe in until my body feels full of light
and i thank the heavens for watching me through my darkest days
and thank them for letting me see today
and i will do this again
every time
until it's all i know

the dream you have is mine too

how can i feel so much for you
at every second of every day
but be at such a loss for any real words
every second of every day

you have taken all my words away
straight from my mouth
all the days before
i felt bound to spill right over
with something like pomegranate
juice
oozing from my lips

now i just want to melt into your
arms
that's all
i don't even want words
i want you

and the dream you have
it's mine
oh it's mine too

audrey ann

laughing is medicine

i laughed for the first time today
at least for the real first time
in a long time
it was the kind that you can't contain
because it had been too long since the last time
so you almost forget how
it just keeps coming and by the time you do stop
you don't even remember why you started

it's like riding a bike for the time without training wheels
your dad lets go and your feet keep pedaling
and your legs wobble up and down
and your hair flies in the wind
and your smile takes up half your face

it felt good to feel that way again
i'd begun to forget myself
i'd begun to forget how to laugh
or feel genuine happiness
or feel genuinely like
me
it felt so nice

and i stopped and i looked around at the faces i was laughing with
i felt so free
i felt so whole
i felt so warm
like this warmth was what i was looking for all this time

the thing was

audrey ann

it was always right before my eyes or right beside me
i had just stopped looking

96

i am a part of the universe

the sun had kissed my cheeks and left red lipstick stains
my skin was sticky
i imagined it was probably sweet like honey
my hair flew
practically dancing behind me
i ran to lay on the grass as it weaved between my fingers
i was soaking in the earth
my body was a magnet and i couldn't move from the ground
i was a part of the universe
i am a part of the universe

audrey ann

this is fourteen

i know, i know so little
i'm learning everyday to let the awkward amount of space
from where i am now and where i want to be
(and sometimes feel i need to be)
not scare me so much
(as it did just last week)

but the truth is
i second guess every letter i've spoken
i move my hand above the side of my scarred cheek
thinking this must be the only thing they see
i won't smile for a week before someone gathers enough laughter
out of my soul for me to show my teeth
i feel awkward and shaky in my bones at times

i think i'm too old for my age
yet sometimes i feel too young
to feel this old
(i'm afraid sometimes that i pressed fast forward on my youth)

but then i turn to my left and there's a giant stuffed animal in my face
(panicked there for a second)

because my tongue is still stained blue from a popsicle
i'm unaware of the world around me
and sometimes i forget to make myself dinner
and i even lack the ability to drive a car

i have a whole entire world waiting for me
a whole world awaiting me to change it

98

audrey ann

i feel liberated now
(and a bit shaky still)

happy days are ahead

the world has been cold and
even a little cruel to me this week
but
i always know in my heart
that happy days are ahead of me

i will learn to take good care of myself again
because i always have

and soon a day will come
when the windows are down
and you're driving
and there's music blasting
and your plans for tomorrow couldn't come soon enough
and you did good today because you put something good in the world
you can taste everything so much more vibrantly and vast then you ever did
before
these are the happy days
they are coming
they are always coming
they may feel in your past but they are also
ahead of you

happy days are ahead
happy days are ahead
happy days are ahead

audrey ann

dear future me

you know how people say
sometimes you feel so cold
so frigid that you're not sure you'll ever be warm again
or that summer will ever come again in the depths of winter
but somehow summer comes and goes
just how when you feel so empty
so sad
that you're not sure you'll ever be happy again
or that you'll ever be able to simply
get out of bed

but somehow you find yourself three month later
laughing your head off with your best friends
and jumping out of bed in the morning
and dancing around your room

that thing

that happens to me a lot
this sense of thinking i'll never quite be alright again
well i don't want to keep forgetting those good moments
the ones where it felt like you paused time and looked around and said
hey look at that
you're doing that one thing that felt so impossible
you're alright
so dear future me, don't forget these things, don't forget these feelings, these
simple accomplishments
dear future me,
don't forget yourself
don't forget your friends

don't forget your family
don't forget what it feels like to laugh your head off
don't forget what it feels like to dance around in your backyard screaming taylor
swift songs with your best friends
don't forget what it feels like to perform
don't forget what it feels like to feel a part of something finally
(you are a part of something... don't talk yourself down)
don't forget what it feels like to love yourself
to finally really love yourself.
and don't forget what it feels like
to be alive

i know that sounds odd

but imagine running through a field in the midst of summer as fast as you can
with the largest smile on your face
thinking
this is it
this is why i'm alive
for this moment alone
i was made to simply feel this whole at some point in my life

not saying i've run through many fields this year
(or really any at all)
but imagine it

you know when you're surrounded by your favorite people
you get this sort of energy from them that builds in your bones, in your heart
or you've just finally finished something that took a lot of effort
or maybe you were so sad for so long and one day you wake up and you finally
feel alright enough to get up again
you notice you feel alive again
don't forget that
don't forget what's it's like to feel alive

to live
to really live
don't forget these things

shaky hands

i believe the universe made us so we could meet
so that i could hold your shaky hands
and hug your tired body
so that i could sort through the pain you tangle in your brain
so that i can be the one you see when you close your eyes at night
no more staring at the ceiling wondering why you're here
you're here because i need your laugh
i need your face
i need your hands
your soul
your mind
your words
you
i need you
because i've laid awake all the same nights wondering why i'm here too
i hung on hoping for someone like you
that means something
that has to mean something

104

you make me believe

i haven't liked myself in awhile
but you make me believe in clichés
the ones i've trained myself *not* to believe
i'm letting myself believe them

i hope i'm not sorry for falling
because now you have me skipping up stairs and humming love songs i don't
even know the words to yet

and i want to melt when i read your words
fall to pieces in your hands
have them touch me
hold me

i dream of you
and i feel butterflies in my legs
it's like your hand is on my thigh

how do you fall for a person you've never met
how do you fall for a person over a screen
i feel the world pulling me back to earth
but you make me want to run and believe in fairytales again

it feels like i've held you in my arms a thousand times
it feels like i've smelled you on my neck
it feels like i've seen you in everything

i tell myself this can't be anything
but you let me be the hopeless romantic i am

audrey ann

so i believe everything

things you deserve

i hope the moon is always visible from your window
i hope songs feel like honey in your throat
i hope the sunlight kisses your cheek for me
i hope the flowers hold your nervous hands
i hope your tears taste sweet
i hope you hear the birds sing i love you's
i hope you only catch the sky when it's pink
i hope you only ever lie in the grass when it's green like my eyes looked that day

"what do you mean?"

you know what this feeling is
it's my heart shattering into pieces like glass
and floating away with the stars

my stomach setting off like fireworks
my arms detaching
my legs going numb
my mouth open waiting for you to kiss it

soon i'm nothing but a heart beating for yours
and a body that's gone in the sky
with the flowers this spring

that's it!
that's the feeling!
it's being in love!

audrey ann

beggar

i've never begged so silently as i did for you

never clung to pages that had nothing to do with me that hard

hung onto words like they were the very air i breathed
when you were only cursing at the moon

i even listened to your music like you were
writing me love letters in them
though you always wrote about golden skin
and long silk hair

i should've known you were never speaking of me when i cut my hair
that june and you called me snow white

i almost lost it in september
when you never called again
but you get lonely in winter
so i got on my scarred knees once more
and praised a love who never really loved me

i could make myself foolishly believe a
million lies you say
if you asked nicely

if you told me you'd finally love me
like i've begged silently for

109

the villain in your story

i always write about the pain others hand me
but i turn right around and give it away

i hurt just as many people
they just don't write poetry about it like i do
they just suffer in silence without a pen
without me knowing

in the end we always hurt people
but it all makes sense in our own forms of poetry

audrey ann

i'll come back

to love you always in a way i will never speak of
coming back to you even after
i've sobbed on the bathroom floor
something in me cannot stay away
something in me always goes back to you

stop lying about me in your 4am poetry

just because i couldn't love you
doesn't make you a victim in your own film

doesn't make me a liar
doesn't make me evil
stop changing my lines
stop making me into the killer

car song

i could watch you in the side-view mirror like
my favorite movie
lay my head on the seat in front of me like
it were your shoulder
yell the lyrics of the song on to the head rest

grab my hand through the window again
i'll hold on longer this time
i was just afraid if i didn't let go then i
wouldn't be able to bring myself to in five more seconds
just five more seconds and you would have had me

what's that feel like
to hold all my senses in your bare hands

113

touch starved

i cried on the bathroom floor staring at the
beige wall like an old friend
the tears that melted down my face
were the warmest touch i've felt in weeks

i don't know my own skin
nobody does
if you won't reach for me
can i
touch your hands
trace my finger down the bridge of your nose
draw stars on your back
place my feet on top of yours
hold you with my arms around your waist
play softly with your hair

i am starving
for a love where we hold hands
a love where i hold you

114

do you feel the world too?

you in the sun
laying on your stomach
my blanket from home
i will never feel the world as much as i do
as when i'm sitting beside you
existing

please
throw your head back laughing one more time
look me in the eyes one more time
hum the words to the song on the radio one more time
touch me one more time

115

trauma bond

i think he really did love me
and i think i could've loved him back

but she hurt me in all the worst ways possible
without even touching me
she killed me in little glances and small
gestures and in her words
oh her words were like knives

and now i can't even let the boy love me
it's so painful
all her knives in my chest
all the sleepless nights
and tear stained pillows i've had to wash over her

she switches on me like a match
comes as quick as it goes
her like a flame
i can't strike her though
she only holds that power over me

and the poor boy just needed some hands to hold and a neck to kiss and some
kind words to get him through the day

she asks for a world i can't supply
though i've tried my best to hold even parts
of the whole earth for her
it's never been enough to make her stay

so i tell the boy i can't love him

audrey ann

because of you

last poem for you

you only liked me because i wrote about you
like a dream
i romanticized you so much you fell in love
with the person i made up for you
you like yourself better in my poetry
admit it
you liked that people loved my words so much
because in a twisted way
people finally loved you

beginning of may

it's late at night
my window is open
a breeze filters through the screen
the world has been grey all day
rain still trickling down my roof into the gutters
birds sing softly to each other
two girls are walking down the street laughing
i'm sure they feel like they're inventing something
my body feels limp
i'm swallowed whole by my bed
i feel tears in my throat
i'm almost touching the stars
i want to feel this hopeful again tomorrow

"platonic"

i loved you before i knew i loved you
and i loved you last year
and i loved you last week
and i love you today
and i will love still even if you never want to look at me again

something in me has to love you
was made to love you
is always searching for you in the room
is always waiting for your laugh
is always wanting you to text me
is always hoping there's a seat left by you
is always happy when you're stuck with me
is always nervous when you look at me a few seconds too long
is always too quick to answer you
is always so excited when you say my name
is always reading to find you in the pages
is always listening to your music to know you more

to think i thought this was nothing before
fool
i have loved you always

and i will love you again tomorrow

cravings

i crave so badly
to trace every one of your fingers

to kiss you while you laugh
so i can hear you echo through my body

to look into your eyes
for so long i mistake them for the ocean

kiss the mountains

we crave an earth not supplied to us
we long for cold air in our lungs
and heat on our shoulders
rocks under foot and dirt in our shoes

how lovely it is to feel connected to something
other than ourselves

do the mountain tops ache for us too
let's be children again
the hills as our playground

silence

i could go on never speaking to you again
if all i had was your heat
the hum of your voice
and the air you breathe
rising and falling in between

audrey ann

alone again

sometimes all i need is my own company
to talk to my own demons
ask them to leave softly
let me have this day
stay away for a couple hours
while i relearn to live with myself

and it's these softest days
alone again
that i remember i need nothing else
but the soft hum of my own voice
a good book
a cup of coffee
and not a soul holding me

i belong to nobody
and this is my peace
i fall asleep with my own hand resting on my face
i'm a mystery to all but myself

nobody waits for me and i wait for no one
my mornings belong to me
and my nights end when my eyes feel heavy
i don't stay up waiting for my screen to glow

there is power in being alone
there is power in making a meal for one

how things are

you look for my eyes
while you laugh in a group

you hug me longer
and linger by the door

i stare at our hands
close enough to touch

my heart swells knowing i went another day
without kissing you
and i miss you already while i'm saying
goodbye

oh let me love you

audrey ann

to the ballerina crying in silence

i know you've looked in the mirror since you were eight and seen a war zone
but you are the only one in this fight dear
please handle yourself with care
when you untangle your hair
look in your bathroom mirror
your tights imprinted on your stomach
trace your frail body
from the bridge of your nose
down to your blistered toes
you are the physical embodiment of grace itself
you are why the audience applauds
and the reason the little girl in the hallway starts classes next month

you don't have to hate yourself you know?
do you remember why you started?
before the world told you who to be

i don't think your ribs are too wide
or your thighs too big
or your arms too fat
you have made eyes water and musicians play and people paint
what's a body but something more to make art with?

to the ballerina crying in silence
i was you many times
but for once i feel powerful in a size large and i don't weigh myself every
morning
and i don't count calories
and i look in the mirror and see a woman
not a child trying to act like one

audrey ann

one day you'll feel normal in your skin again
one day you won't be crying in silence

audrey ann

closing love letter

I want to thank my mom for helping me edit these poems and for always supporting and pushing my dreams. I may not have ever believed I could actually put this together if it wasn't for you. I love you mom, always.

Thank you to my best friends for being inspirations to many of these poems. I can't even begin to count the number of nights I drive home with a smile plastered on my face after one of our performances or late night ice cream runs. You all constantly bring light and love and laughter into my life when I need it the most. I love you guys forever.

Thank you to all the lovers who never loved me back. I grew because of you, and I'm not sure where I'd be without the pain and confusion you brought into my life. Maybe this book wouldn't even be here right now. I have made my best art because of you. May you live on in these pages but never again in my heart.

Lastly I want to thank all the people who have followed me since the very beginning, and even the people who followed me last week. I owe everything to you, none of this would be happening if you hadn't given me the chance. 2018 is when I uploaded my first visual poetry video. My whole body was shaking and I honestly wanted to throw up pressing publish. After that it got easier and easier to share more of my writing. What I've learned the most on the internet is that you have to give people the chance to be good to you. Someone out there needs your voice. Take chances and make things you're passionate about.

I started on the internet at twelve and at a very dark time in my life when I didn't like who I was. I found an escape in creating for you all and making pretty things. To have even just this small platform and fanbase now is incredible. I feel like I've just about grown up with some of you. From the beginning to now, thank you for supporting me and now my writing. I feel like I'm making that twelve year old girl proud.

Love, Audrey Ann

about the author

Audrey is a seventeen year old Youtuber, Instagram Poet, and ballerina. This is her debut poetry book. She currently lives in Kansas and has homeschooled all throughout her life. Audrey started her Youtube channel, Audrey Ann, in September of 2015 by making ballet and makeup related videos. She now focuses more on film and lifestyle content. Audrey enjoys baking vegan desserts, listening to classical music while lying in the grass, going antiquing for vintage treasures, hosting extravagant sleepovers for her best friends, reading sad romance novels, and watching sad romance movies.

@audreyaann

www.ingramcontent.com/pod-product-compliance
Lightning Source LLC
Chambersburg PA
CBHW062214150726
47991CB00006B/2273